VOLUME 2

The Return of the Unconventional CEO

MORE LESSONS ON COMMON SENSE,
IDEAS ON GETTING MORE OUT OF
YOUR POSITION
AND FINDING YOUR CEO MOJO

MARIO PRETORIUS

First Edition, 2020

ISBN: 978-1-77605-665-1

Produced by Kwarts Publishers
www.kwartspublishers.co.za

Contact the author:
Mario Pretorius
www.mariopretorius.co.za
Mobile: +27 836412000
mp@valcapital.co.za

The Unconventional CEO has done it again!

Only in very rare instances the sequel exceeds the original masterpiece.

The Return of the Unconventional CEO is an oasis of wisdom for everyone with a true thirst for insight into life's more complicated matters.

The book packs a powerful punch. Concise and crisp, it challenges and disarms conventional believes.

A guide for up-and-coming CEOs, a reference for seasoned CEOs and once acquainted, a trusted friend to revisit annually.

Francois du Plessis
CEO, Vega Capital, Pretoria

In Battle better
a Stout HEART
than a Sharp
SWORD

CONTENTS

INTRODUCTION

The 2017 self-publication of The Unconventional CEO had some highlights. A number of CEOs ordered cases of copies for their staff. Three media houses serialised the book. Great feedback came from Economics students after I handed each a freebie after guest lectures. It gave me some vindication for the effort to hear colleagues referring to passages that inspired them to revert to using common sense. I set out to have fun and rekindle the lessons that I never found in business books.

Here's more of the same but on a more irreverent note. One sees what one is looking for and I found some more ideas and lessons. I hope these trigger the dormant lessons you might have learned too.

Mario Pretorius
Bakoven, 2020

Mario Pretorius' Biography

So far my luck is holding out. I have spent a lifetime preparing for things that may never happen; the peaceful revolutions and the earth-shattering theories. On the way, I picked up an MBA from the Graduate School of Business (GSB) in Cape Town and attended some postgraduate courses at the GSB, as well as Harvard Business School. My working experience includes multiple-year stints in Oslo, Milwaukee, Toledo and Ann Arbor, Michigan.

My corporate life included the very large (South African Breweries), the large (Malbak Subsidiaries) and the medium. I have listed three companies on the Johannesburg Stock Exchange (JSE Ltd). Because, but mostly in spite of, my best efforts, I have succeeded in business in multiple disciplines as founder and owner, across various industries, from property development to telecommunications. Through the Junior Chamber of Commerce I visited many countries, made lifelong friends and acquired an appetite for learning and understanding. After I fired myself as CEO of TeleMasters into the Chairmanship, I hoped a restless soul would settle. Forays into multiple-country farming, marine diamond mining, (more) property development, data center building and a child-feeding programme means there is some life left in the dog.

My full bio is on LinkedIn and on Who's Who. You can follow me on Twitter here: @unconCEO. My website is www.MarioPretorius.co.za. Please feel free to contact me.

DEDICATION

Life is a hard taskmasters and some say that the consequences are lessons, not failures. There are the joys of small achievements and wishes come true that overshadows the disappointments. I dedicate this manuscript to the many sets of eyes that followed my progress, some with a touch of invigorating malice and a few with undeserved kindness, often unexpectedly so.

Close family, close friends and close enemies give balance to a tumultuous life. Thanks to you, I have ventured beyond my self-imposed limits with this 2nd volume in the series.

Dear CEO

In the stillness of the pandemic of 2020 some more thoughts and experiences bubbled up, I do hope you find some sustenance of your long road under your heavy burden. Unsung heroes all you unconventional CEO's, moving the world of commerce forward toward a better quality of life for the fellow travelers following in the caravan – I salute you.

Please browse the following chapters at your leisure, they are in so particular order. If any of the thoughts makes you nod sagely, please share and I will have the satisfaction of having nudged you common sense.

1.

EVERYTHING CAN BE SOLVED IN 5 STEPS OR LESS

This is not a law, but a guide to engage your thinking and skill-solving cortex. The heart of this is that you absolutely must start at basic principles. Want to solve the education crisis? First principle: what is the desired outcome of education? If it is to develop a responsible, economically useful member of a productive community, the first step then, is to structure a timeline where every graded step is a functional step towards the targeted outcome. Want to solve Africa's electricity shortage? First principle first!

The thinking and analysis to get to the correct and appropriate basic principle is hard, but necessary. What you may find may not be pretty or Politically Correct and may cost you in the sanity stakes, but delusional thinking probably got you into the mess you're trying to resolve.

First you should practice on some really deep but abstract stuff to get the process going. How do we stop wars? Wars are the political coward class' way of bullying without much personal cost. General Moshe Dayan said for Israel to protect itself, it 'must be like a mad dog, too dangerous to bother'. The first premise is to let people know you are better left alone.

The second step is to make sure that the pain which will result from not being left alone is a proper deterrent for the other side. Even crippled Zimbabwe kept away its neighbours and the UN by embracing the diamond-lusting Chinese.

The third step is to make conquest unprofitable.

The fourth step is to psyche the population, to keep up its resistance and to appear unconquerable, or at least make it extremely painful to try a war stunt. Consider the reputation of the Gurkhas in

Nepal, the presence of assault rifles in every Swiss home, or Finnish stubbornness. Prevention is better than mobilization.

What is the bedrock for perfect education? For political stability? Could it either be home-maker mothers or no female votes?

That's how deep the first principles go. The rest is Nobel Prize territory.

2.

People are criminally inefficient

There it is: penned by the incomparable and outlandish American artist writer Miles Mathis. It is a first principle of business interaction. Get a machine, a process to do the job. Better still, get the customer to self-provide the service i.e. order online etc. by his own inefficient ways but keep human hands away from tasks, unless you want delays, procrastination, overthinking, wayward actions and every known and often novel foible that homo sapiens can foist on a simple, reciprocally valuable transaction between consenting adults in business.

We may be dealing with *homo inefficio*, the interloper that retards and threatens the transaction, or its execution. The future of business is tied to greater efficiencies, with or without *sapiens sapiens* in employment. Top management thinks itself immune to AI and similar pre-emptive trouble preventers. It may not be so and pulling the strings after calling the shots could be limited to making the coffee and oiling the fans of the machine of its young coding genius that crunched big and small data into manageable chunks for lesser-paid managers.

Your type may not be trusted any longer to make irrefutable decisions, based on old ideas and on guessed-at data that had previously been inaccessible to you. You probably are also one of those people Mathis is referring to, the criminally inefficient despite your whopping salary. If you are, surely some geek is aiming at you as a trophy too?

This is bad news, even for an Unconventional CEO. How will you overcome this? How do you cement the power of your irrevocable decisions? There could be sleepless nights ahead.

3.

Selling 'subject to the board', but sign now

So much time is wasted and so many opportunities are lost in the delay of corporate decision-making. A small commitment is the invaluable first shuffle to success. Waiting for a 'big bang' where everything happens at once is just a frustrating fantasy. Selling involves incremental steps of trust and consequent commitment. 'Subject to' is a neat test of where the trust level lies in a sale. If the buyer seems keen, ask for his signature. If he defers, agree to a 'subject to his boss' approval'. He must then share the responsibility to convince Mr Big.

No John Hancock forthcoming from Mr Buyer means you're not even at first base. Words and promises don't cut it. Keep building trust and keep lowering risk for at least the 'subject to' commitment. The point here is to reach and then maintain momentum instead of waiting for 'One giant leap for Mankind' sometime later. With small moves, cumulative progress, the tango is on – and the smooth rhythm is found without the lady's toes getting crushed.

This is literally that 'One Small Step for a Man' on the mission to conquer.

4.

Rat poison people

Rat poison is very edible. It's the less than 1% warfarin, a huge poison overdose, that will stop coagulation and induce a slow, horrible end. Ditto dangerous people. They too are 99% sweetness & light but with a toxic streak. How do you spot them? Any driver can steer a straight road, so put them around the bends to see the stress reaction. Poisonous people will protect only themselves. It's the empathy types that you need to 'bind to your soul with hoops of steel' as old Polonius advised his son Laertes in Shakespeare's Hamlet.

Good luck and good riddance with spotting and weeding out these types. They practice their deception more diligently than you would in sniffing it out. There may be a little rat hiding in most people, waiting for the right circumstances to appear. Only a few Lords like you get this absolutely right but beware the tiny hole that can sink a ship. Heed the scent of almonds – that can indicate arsenic – and act Machiavellian.

Never allow destructive people a second chance – or they will leap at the next chance to poison you.

5.

What someone knows vs what they can do is problematic

Well known thinker and author of The Black Swan, Nassim Nicholas Taleb separates Slave Drivers from the Free Man in one easy observation: Slave Drivers abdicate the execution to Slaves and trust it would be done. Only Free Men can do, when necessary, whatever needs to happen at all levels. The 'answers' exist and answers can be agreed upon. Executing them on the fly and under ever-changing conditions without having to delegate, is tricky.

The knowledgeable Free Man is limited to what he can decide on an issue. Answers are only real solutions once completed and effective. Beware of he who cannot transform his ideas into working actions. Be the Free Man – this needs deep understanding of the empire you preside over. Go get yourself into the beast's belly and figure out what is being done as well as what should have been done.

Many will know what the perfectly executed operation looks like but may not be able to stamp their glorious mark on such an outcome. Their inability is waiting for your guidance and resolution. It could be the following sequence: Understand first what should be done, then what can be done, and question what is being done. Guide them to close the gap between knowing what to do and completing the task. Execution counts, ideas are, well, only wishes. There is great personal satisfaction all around when the thinkers become doers and get good at that.

Your satisfaction should be the greatest of all, Good Leader.

6.

Do you believe your own memes?

Don't we just love our own proverbs? Such as 'the first sales guy in front of the customer will get the sale'. Or 'The market is post-dividend; it is ready for share growth'. Do you subscribe to such Corporate Wisdom? Is it still true and valid – was it ever so? Just how much do these home truths shape and misguide the path towards success? Each of us believes a set of guidelines – you had better state them and test them thoroughly.

It may be time to re-calibrate your jungle-cutters through a soul-baring confession of My Innermost Memes. Is laying optic fibre a real-estate grab? Is mining in terminal decline? Should you ever appoint anyone under 30?

There are many of these casual clichés that become 'principles' in business as accepted wisdom. It may be for mysterious reasons or just by the Top Dog's repetition as gospel truth and requoted in the hallways as The Man's wisdom. Now list them – or ask your handy lieutenants to help you do so – and then test each for accuracy and truth. It's bloody, but bloody liberating.

You may be right and correct. You may find that new memes should replace the untrue. For added spice, do the same for your competitors' mantra, and you will better understand their mis-shapen trudging. Some of these may survive and emboss your reputation as a younger Odin with both eyes open.

Hopefully you will not have to sacrifice one eye for wisdom like he did.

7.

DIRECT COMMAND OR ADHOCRACY

Command & Control, or delegation of authority? Frankly, neither is optimal. There is not enough time and energy to C&C from the top to the bottom. From the Big Boss to 2IC to Line Boss to the Supervisor – how can all issues be solved at your level and then commanded for execution to subordinates? There aren't enough hours in the day or caffeine in your bloodstream. Ditto the Goals & Own Actions model – this needs the endless time of Quality Control by good supervision.

All this is just academic nonsense. In your enterprise most things will work on an Adhocracy concept – your talented staff just do what is needed and you will make decisions to fix breakdowns on an *ad hoc* basis. Hell yes! It inevitably has unintended consequences, but with the flashing neon in their heads that mistakes must be fixed where and when they are made, you should relax. If they know the destination, they will find the way.

Try telling a builder how to do his job better. Or an architect. Even your dentist. Get the picture? The pair of hands entrusted to the task is best at executing it, mostly on an *ad hoc* basis. Establish a safe but responsible environment, then call this style whatever you wish.

'Look & Trust' is probably apt.

8.

ADVANTAGE VS STRATEGY. TACTICS VS GOALS

Another book on 'Strategy' will probably push the world over sanity's edge. Strategy is something to be studied, imbibed, practised, refined, tried – and respected for the hard taskmaster it is.

Read W.E. Hart's 'Hitler's Generals" or "1001 Battles" by R.G. Grant and you will realise that all your strategies are pitted against a multitude of active and aggressive opponents who are defending territory and attacking your efforts. It's 4-dimensional chess and the one saving grace that keeps you alive is that almost everyone is pitifully useless at good strategy. Your strategy should be based on the advantages you've built: better tanks, more planes, faster debt collection for cash. Don't have these? Sell the business & leave the stage while you still breathe.

You must, absolutely must manifest a clear and unambiguous advantage that swings the customer's mind and makes him fire his current suppliers. Be more the hunting lion and less a scavenging hyena; hunts are where the real action is. Goals without strategy and without advantages is pure hope. The WHAT you are going to do to press home an overpowering advantage on a decisive point (that's from Prussian military strategist Carl Von Clausewitz) is crucial to victory. The implementation of your advantage is your tactic: daily, hourly, by each moment. Where can you use it? What advantages do you have at hand? Which new ones should you acquire and how can that help you get the edge?

Tactics must often be adapted. Your low prices may have been copied. The extended guarantee became too expensive or the handing out of match tickets are suddenly frowned upon by clients' bosses. New advantages are required and your management must innovate a larder of these, ready to be thrown into battle.

Goals may vary or become imprecise but having goals other than getting and staying ahead of the competition whilst generating operating cash is distracting. Nature is relentless about favouring advantage. Diversity and choice are repeated until the most advantageous tactics triumph. 'Occam's Razor' rules too; keep it simple, stick to the uncomplicated. That is an advantage by itself.

9.

Speedocution

Here's an anomaly. In days of analogue technology, life was rather simple: focus and then perform. In the 80's we newly minted MBAs just kicked up fancy-dust in a millennia-old system of trading favours, wrapped around products, for cash. Nowadays the same applies – but the volume of distractions is overwhelming. It's hiding in the big data. You should know the minimum of what you want to learn via digital compilation of the outputs in your business. Variations in tyre pressure? Changes in the browsing patterns of the store clerks? Bond yields by the hour where your cash is silently earning? The quantum is a deluge. Beware paralysis by analysis. Or worse – Procrastination from Contemplation is as deadly to momentum.

Deep breaths: there is an enormity of information that is worth knowing and which conspires to affect the future. The better your dashboard the more you will want to know and often to more decimal digits of accuracy. What affects your business directly in advance? How do you know it has been affected? How can you be sure the remedies are working? This circle of Q&A must be kept small and tight for Speedocution – acting early and adapting the actions to perfection.

Every department must have its early warning information and damage / accolades report. What to measure and how accurate, how often and how timely is the feedback? Perfecting the data mining into a competitive advantage is a great insurance against surprises. It's more rear-view mirror than headlights driving. The trajectory into future impacts must guide the course adjustment. What does it mean? Is it vital? – must be the benchmark questions for arranging the dashboard.

Why Speedocution? FOFUD (Fear of F*cked-up Decisions) must be banished. Make them, re-make them, and keep making them on a moment-to-moment basis. Don't bet the farm – plant more and plant better. SPEEDING from idea to execution will ensure that you make all the necessary mistakes, learn from them and fix them. No-one bats perfectly; batting poorly comes from too little batting practice.

The mined information is bowling at you and your team. With enough swings you should be clipping the boundary very often.

10.

TIMELINE EVERY TACTIC

"When? Why not now?" This should be your management rallying-cry. Time is of the utmost essence and more so as each day passes. Missed deadlines are unforgiveable and you must treat them severely. Execs and their staff must competently plan, budget and timeline the implementation and outcomes of tactics and other actions. A deadline is a hell-or-highwater commitment that fits into the overarching strategy. Whomever signs off on the deadline must deliver and do whatever is necessary in a timely manner to bring the tactic to fruition.

Every tactic must be properly set in time, both reasonable and achievable. A single missed delivery deadline can push an entire project towards the cliff and impact on all other pending actions. Think nuclear power station building cost overruns. Your staff must know and understand that unless they reach the Light in time, the Heat will descend as that other type of persuasion. Your hand should be felt in the executability of important steps in the tactical process. Is the implementation doable with the resources – including the competence of the team? Are their novel ideas required for success?

Technological and other changes have overwhelmed us, and the threats that confronted the Luddites* are a thousand-fold greater now as we enter an age of the machines competing in unimaginable ways. Your brief, shining moments of Glory, where brilliant advantages can be exploited, will before very long be threatened by someone else's Even Better Idea.

Thankfully, it still takes about a decade for technology ideas to mature and to win general acceptance. But I bet that this slow pace won't last. Nowadays, a new App can storm the world in under a

---

*18th Century secret society that destroyed automation

week. Best that you hurry up and enforce your brilliance on a hungry clientele before daybreak, for fear that foot-dragging will mean that your resignation speech will precede it. Think. Plan. Act soonest with an irrevocable deadline. It's War out there and they take no prisoners on rations in Capitalism, bud.

11.

Humouring the changes

Cracking the introvert's shell doesn't come easily – but cracking a smile does. Corny or not – pithy humour is a great lubricant in setting something straight. In fact, you are telling someone they screwed up while being paid and that a better way of doing has to be found – or else. Humour relieves the tensions of the burning self-recriminations of your Best & Brightest who have failed to match your lofty, but oh so achievable, expectations of them.

Don't dwell on the past, except to acknowledge its impact and giving them a short pause to spend the emotional energy on recharging their Tesla'd-out batteries. "Hope the next idea will cost less than the four Porsches I lost with this one," is a one-liner that contains enough menace wrapped in humour – if said with a smile.

You too, are part of every screw-up because you trusted them. You too must retreat to the mirror to remonstrate with your ill judgement. Just fix the circumstances quietly. They must know that your benevolence exceeds your dismay, but that your expectation of their future perfection is now a double-or-quits bet.

Don't destroy the remorseful; a single look will sear their souls and you want their uncooked flesh to do better next time.

12.

RETURN OF CAPITAL AND RETURN ON CAPITAL

You shake the poker dice and are ready to roll – or are you? In putting together the project, you should ensure that the backstop is firm and the minimum goal is the return **OF** capital, as my friend Russel admonishes. Stuff happens – more often that we would like, and far more frequently, too. The problem is that the unpredictable gods of chance are not invited but turn up anyway. Things unravel, the centre buckles – so what's the exit plan?

Capital is hard to accumulate – especially after expenses, tax, and the payment of dividends. This is a precious reminder of the 99% turnover that you had to mine to find the carat of 1% return on capital. Capital must not be squandered; it must be protected, must be risked with a good stop-loss position. It gets worse when there is loan capital in the game; somehow human nature then allows the seeds of impunity to be cast into the wind. Returns remain the joy of the spreadsheet.

When computing the return ON capital, always contemplate and protect the return OF capital. Someone worked really hard to accumulate it too.

13.

YES, BUT VS NO, BUT

You have asked an important question. Listen carefully to the answer. You have to discern the Closed Door from the Inviting Concerned. Both may sound the same to the untrained ear, but to you, the Unconventional CEO, it is obvious. The 'NO-BUT' means No – and you cannot reason your way out of it. The YES-BUT leaves a door open. It is essentially a NO but with an added opportunity to clarify and convince. The NO-BUT will keep on putting up a new defence of 'no' as soon as you answered the previous issue. Its price, then it's delivery time and then it's something else – let it go.

A key question to discern the two types is:

'Are these all the concerns you have? If I can answer all of them, can we move forward?'

The NO-BUT will dismiss the idea. NO-BUT is closed negative. They do not want what you offer and none of your arguments will persuade. NO-BUT's mind is made up and hostile. You will be wasting your time. Leave.

You need to probe carefully when encountering a 'no'. Probe, question until YES-BUT emerges. YES-BUT is movement and not dismissal, it asks for more information, needs you to prove trustworthiness and benefit. You may continue the search for the elusive 'yes' and you are on friendly territory.

A 'Pattern Interrupt' may help – something completely unexpectedly done to break the NO-BUT stand-off. You must prepare this in advance for its effective use. "We have charted a plane to see the test on Saturday in Cape Town. Why don't you and your wife join us and then you can see if we have common ground. Our limo will pick you up in the morning".

Don't push on a string if they don't understand your offer; educate them gently towards understanding.

Some are the *Immovables*, some are *Movables* and then there is you: the *Mover*.

14.

Listening to glib opinions instead of to the hard truth

Brave is the man and rare, who can step out of his cage and see his world as it is. He who has this courage, whose underlings are fearless enough to bring the stark reality home that his product sucks and his services stink? We can gloss over our pimple-speckled teen acting if she's our beauty queen, but what happens when the sales don't bear it out? Care for the glib answers and excuses, promises of better-next-time and other ego-supporting flattery? She's a dog and you need to be told that and confront it.

Take a deep breath and let's face it; even Porsche screws up. Look at the poor reviews for the Panamera. Remember the underwhelming Porsche 924 and the much-despised diesel Cayenne SUV? At some point some soul, brave and true, raised a hand in the lull after the self-congratulatory hubbub with a searing question. The world – and Porsche – is a better place for that. Ditto Apple, and Boeing, and Coke – and so on down the Alphabet.

Your chances of a redeeming, ego-shedding wake-up call lies in the size of those pendulous swinging *cajones*. Look for and find the hard truths. You need to know if there are warts on the snout or lipstick on your pig. Let no opinion sway you from brutal reality.

Be the man that confronts reality and overcomes it with courage.

15.

DON'T COMPETE WITH COMPETITORS; COMPETE FOR THEIR CUSTOMERS

Seems obvious? Obviously not. You should focus on something that the lady wants instead of trying to man-up against the hunk she's with. Compete for the client, not against the competition. You can try to cater for her choices, even if they're not always coherent, rational or consistent. Flout your honed advantage. Get her in the mood. Give her choices. Promise her satisfaction. She has whims. Why would you want to argue with the muscle if you can persuade her with your velvet voice? You had better have something better on show – so get going!

More is known about the competition and their offers than about the customer's wants. Competitor moves are easier seen and watched. Customers are petulant about their desires. Still, customers belong to no-one. Despite this, each and every vendor wants to be the one to tie them in to gut-rupturing long-term incentive contracts. Customers are tied to their latest choices and these are often hinged on crappy offers and dependent on a host of interpersonal trust magic being at play before the signing. Like a relationship, a deal endures only in the absence of harsh light and good competition. Are affairs real? Do divorces even happen? You betcha! – things change, and expectations diverge from signature date onwards.

At least in failure you will know what the client settled for, and what the chances are of seduction into something better, later. You don't have to beat the competition. You just have to be the first to deeply understand what will bring satisfaction and closure to the customer, so you can speedily satisfy, and then grasp that opportunity. Remember the Unmentionables will be after your clientele too, so strengthen and reinforce the reasons they chose you, and you alone in the first place.

Knowing what the competition is up to is essential but knowing what will ink the contract at the customer is vital.

16.

CEO: A POSITION OR A FUNCTION WITH MULTIPLE EXTERNAL HELP?

It baffles me that large company CEOs get paid the astronomical dues they demand. Are they worth it? All by themselves? In my time, *moi* was the lowliest paid of all listed-company CEOs on the JSE. Peanuts. It even dropped by a third when we had to lay off some good people. Our worth lies in convincing others to do what we think best and cannot do ourselves.

How would you turn around, say, a struggling utility like South Africa's electricity giant Eskom? It had nine CEOs in eleven years, but it's still doomed. Here's a plan: put out a bid for the top functions. Bring your Team – not just yourself but your CFO, CTO and COO. The CEO pay is R9.1m per annum. The other functions will together require another R15million annually. It would be a total package of about R2m a month for you and your Team. It's your project for five years.

Consultants, experts – there must be no restriction on the number of external helpers you can get on board your Team to get the job done. Rotate them at will, but get the job done – it must be in your monthly budget. If the Team doesn't get results, the whole Team has to go, not only parts of it.

There is a level of worth in the expertise that you, a single individual, can give constantly, in the same working hours as mere mortals. Accept that it's not higher than the output of a dedicated, ego-less team – outside the limelight of the self-importance of the All-Knowing Me. And the C-Suite is generally just that: past-prime delegators, afraid of the hard decisions that will impact nurtured legacies of the Permanently Imbedded.

This could become the real gig economy – functions, not people. Such roving Top Gun teams could be the future and a very effective one too.

17.

FAILURE IS NOT THE ENEMY, BUT SUCCESS IS!

It saps the ambition, mollifies the hunger, and dulls the ambition when self-congratulatory indulgence leads you to believe that the 'goal' is reached and 'rewards' are in order.

Thus, momentum is lost, opportunities missed and the mission stalls. Guard against taking respite. Failure is a hard taskmaster, but success is an insidious trap for the unwary. How many moments do you need to bask with the laurel wreath around the neck? How many swigs from the champagne on the podium?

Must the Yellow Jersey be taken seriously at all? Better be humble in success, be magnanimous in the spotlight, be supportive of the many hands that pulled that shining chariot over the firmament in triumph.

Success is not permanent. Like the plucked rose it starts withering immediately. Hard Times make Strong People. Strong People make Good Times. Good Times make Weak People. Weak People make Hard Times. Such is the cycle.

The Chinese proverb of wealth destruction is 'from paddy to paddy in three generations' – success is very difficult to maintain over multiple generations. You need to stay hungry and your wolfpack needs to be even more so in order to keep up the survival rate and test and weed the new leaders.

Failure gives rise to lessons; success gives bragging rights. Which is better in the marathon of Life?

Fear the consequences of success as you will be less focussed on attaining it than when striving for glory in your darker days.

18.

How men function

We are so predictable, or so they say.

A man has two bulges in his pants that may bother him. One is his wallet. The other is more anatomical. The problem arises when the wrong one is full or empty. Of course, ideally the wallet should be the filled-up item. Men would empty that for a double discharge. It's easy to understand; we spend a lifetime doing this spend/spent routine.

Women would a the double-take of this. This is crude analogy. Do men really function at such a base level? Perhaps this is only true of the Alpha males. Soy Boy territory could have its own rules. Why is this important to know? We're tribal creatures, forever in domination games and pretty simple minded. How are we bribed? Girls and money. How can it be so easy? Two bulges.

How do Women function? No idea, except to suggest that … nah, that will just be speculation. Professionally speaking the advent of the Lady Boss has played havoc with gender rules and behaviours; in 50 years of observation the tumult has not subsided and if anything, the glass ceiling/gender wars have some way to go. Let's not get comfortable with calling the presiding officer a piece of padded furniture instead of by the correct title: Chairman.

19.

Recovery

'The greatest mistake a man can ever make is to be afraid of making one' said Elmar Hubbard. Just idle talk, easily dismissed? Surely you have some horror stories of your own? What's to learn from the smoking wreck of a well-intended strategy?

Lots. Instead of a life-long resentment analysis, ask just one question: what single but crucial piece of information did I miss that would have stopped me from making the wrong decision? Spare yourself finding the correct decision that could have saved the day; just focus on the 'I really should have thought of THAT' which would have prevented your ignominious debut as a Harvard Case Study.

Bad choice of jockey? What did you miss? Why? Here's a Recovery Question, then: What should you have known about him that you missed? 'The competitor's reaction was unforeseen?' Recovery Question: What should I have known about their margins that prompted them to cut prices too much?

Learn from your beauts so you make fewer in future. Ask the recovery question and take the lessons to heart, business careers are intolerant to making habits of disasters. Or like Harry Potter said: 'Rather cleverer than most men, my mistakes tend to be correspondingly bigger'. Fix your boo-boo's before you polish them for display at the 19th hole.

As my friend Francois muses: 'If you make an expensive mistake, make sure you get value for your money'.

20.

THE MATURITY AGE OF PEOPLE

Most of us don't feel our age. 'A 19-year-old in a 59-year-old body,' is what the youngsters don't understand of this wrinkled wreck before them. Feeling much younger than you are explains why most of us then get stuck at a certain, often inappropriate, maturity level, too.

It is important to look into the eyes and determine the mental age of their owner. It's generally between nine and say, twenty-nine where maturity and responsibility fuse. What age person do you see approximately? Is it the pre-puberty kid? Truculent teenager? Over-confident 19-year old? Uncertain young adult? Smooth Main Man on Campus?

At the other end of the scale, the never-ageing ones can act grown-up when the chips are down and the hackles are up. The real maturity shines through, never mind the baldness or saggy parts. The physiological age can and does fool. It is often the young ones that are mistaken about the codgers, to their own disadvantage.

Oldies weren't born that way; they earned their silver status. Looking into the loving eyes of gramps and grandma does not prepare anyone for the shock of a well-versed and experienced twenty-six-year-old, camouflaged amongst much older sinews. Unfortunately for all of us, many – or even most – people do not age past a more junior point. Thus, the tragedy is that they respond to and can be commanded like they were that age again and also, sadly, that they will never become fine wine.

Judge your opposite number on this.

21.

PHRASE QUESTIONS TO IMPLY THAT THE ANSWER IS ACCEPTABLE

"Please send me any amendments before Mon at 9:00, after which we will implement."

This cunning little time-saver aces the delay tactics. You're on the front foot, setting the agenda and directing the flow towards your idea of the Deal. Practice this. An objection might arise over the stated date. Or the stated time. Both of which can be easily overcome – the objection of the timing is a lightning rod away from the objection to the continuation.

Point is that there's constructive detail that sugar-coats the call to commitment. "Never ask a question that you don't know the answer to," Peter Boyle's character advised political wannabe Robert Redford in The Candidate film. Robert listened and won, a timely lesson for your question-asking abilities too.

Shape, guide, corral, tame and own the other party through your questions. Ask pertinently for answers containing the precision you need, and you must take full advantage if this to get things moving and keep them rolling. Answer questions with questions of your own for deeper understanding. Keep shaping the conversation in your direction by your answers. Keep at it and you may well understand your counter party a lot better.

22.

DRUGS

You are a walking experiment, so it's good to get yourself the best chance to 'suck the cess' of the success you're craving. The interplay between Oxytocin and Vasopressin and the occasional kick-in of the endorphin receptor can be enhanced at the peril of those against you. These hormones are lying in wait for your command or activation via your choice of stimulants.

Endurance sport, neurotropics, health supplements, micro dosing, magic mushrooms and alcohol are …

These are all drugs in the widest sense that you may be able to handle for the correct reasons: improving yourself, and not for the temporary, lifting effect on your psyche.

It takes a certain personality type to get hooked, says Johan Hari in 'Chasing the Scream', a book on the negative impact of drugs. The rest of us, a staggering 95%, can cruise through the experimentation unscathed. Still, there are benefits of nicotine (almost instant emotion reversal, the only substance that switch states to the opposite) and other fringe kicks that you may find beneficial *if under control*.

Live your life as a Totem Pole, be seen as the spiritual guide for your acolytes, but make your drug-fuelled magic while no-one watches. Get the best out of your body and your mind. If you feel the compulsion to abuse it, go easy on the stimulants. You're a spirit, you have a body and it must carry you through this life as long as you can direct and improve it. It is your mind that drives your performance, so artificial help should not be needed or wanted as it will diminish the sense of achievement.

Lance the cyclist can testify to this.

23.

LEARN *@BREAKNECK*

Compare a mountain bike with a stationary cycle. If you chose death-defying, sure-to-be-bloody outdoorsy over secure and repetitive progress, you become truly alive. It's out there at 60km/hour downhill that learning *@breakneck* starts: about praying, avoiding hidden ruts, balance and the afterlife. The uncomfortable bits are stimuli for your 'fight' syndrome – that will not only keep you alive but will kick your guts into a higher gear for survival and proper, real, life-relevant learning. Dirty and bloody, sweaty and scary is the ride. And relentless are the obstacles. Real learning happens away from the screen, the closed door and the campus.

It's face-to-face with enraged customers, a devious opposition, immoral suppliers and mindless financiers. It's being the shotgun rider for the sergeant you entrusted these tasks to, and you are watching his back in person from time to time. You've bypassed the filters that scrub such encounters of their real meaning and set them down in corporate speak. See it for yourself, Tarzan.

Be in the front line where there's trouble – first as the backup until the fruit threatens the fan. Let your people learn to grip the python barehanded; they must grow as well. Magically, they should do a lot better having you as an impressionable audience – so don't spoil it by chipping in.

The ride is glorious but let them do the hard pedalling first. Enjoy!

24.

THE BEST WAY OF GETTING ...

Marrow from a marrow bone ... is with a straw. Unconventional thinking; great results. You have to 'learn faster' from the world around you and make uncommon learning associations. If not, your own learning will stay isometric: tired you'll get and stationary you'll stay.

The gifted around you need little nudges and winks to work out the best way of tackling the forces of evil which are stacking up against you: bad debtors, wavering customers, internal inefficiencies, obsolete systems, lackadaisical implementation and all the horrors your varsity textbooks warned you about.

The fight is on and it's relentless and deadly. If you find the best way, it is heaven. Just opposing the castle gate-bashers with your current armaments could be hell. Best then fire up the internal race to find the 'bestest' ways and then better them: damnation is a horrible end to a brilliant career.

25.

UNIFORMITY OR EXPERIMENTATION?

It's just so typical of the Minion class to standardise everything for the sake of uniformity, or so-called efficiency. Electricity flows at light speed; complexity doesn't faze it. Only, people's knickers go *koeksister* twirl into a twist when deviation is required. Flexibility and lightness on the feet, enables adaptation. Remember evolution: variety, then selection. How to produce variety? Try, fail, try, fail better.

Few strategies require a Moon-shot or a Hail Mary – the football hope-for-success last wild throw in the game by the Quarterback downfield to imaginary receivers. Test and try out. Your successes will be regimented soon after this, into uniformity, because that is how it must be managed. The leadership part is the try-out, the grinding before the polishing, the poking for weaknesses that may cause collapse from inefficiency.

Your tower is built on uniformity but designed by experimentation. Where are you heading in turbulent times, in changing circumstances, in a vibrant market? Surely not the same trajectory as before? What would be the correct change of course, and would you rather experiment with possibilities than yank the rudder when the flight runs into dangerous territory?

Invest in the maybe's and in the what-if's and roll back where necessary. The future isn't completely dark but feeling your way should be a safer option than bursts of blind-folded speed when compelled under pressure.

26.

Bullshit jobs

Some time back, this term didn't even exist. We thought it was rational that functions needed people to execute them. Tomorrow, we will measure the execution of tasks carried out by machines, by systems, by elimination. You just read 'People are criminally inefficient most of the time'. Yet life moves on.

Let this be your morning mantra: "Find the Talent". Obviously, you can view your staff that way. Exceptional performers? Perhaps – but compared to what other method of execution? It is a slowly waning idea that the major component of competitive business is dominantly a social contract with its workers.

Do those who 'Work' – and do not necessary 'Do Business' – make money? The low-level clerical, the shifting of paper, the 'support' or accounting musical chairs. There are real BS jobs out there – unnecessary, as well as soul-destroying. We're out of the Victorian era but now stuck in the work-is-typing-on-a-laptop idea. Why? Why? Systemise; re-think the workflow.

What are *your* people doing that your supplier should be doing and you are needlessly duplicating it in some way?

People must support the system and make it go faster; they must not BE the system. Consider pre-paid or web portal instead of an outdated accounting package. Walk around and wonder: if that was you at that desk, would you be happy doing that? Is that a BS job – unnecessary, uneconomic, demeaning? What perpetuates the creation of these positions?

27.

CLEVER 40; WISE 50; WILY 60

When you get to Old Coyote status, you'll agree we get old too soon and smart too late. So, it is a slow process for knowledge to evolve into wisdom, like ageing good whiskey. At around 60 years, something magical happens to barrelled water-of-life, but don't wait until then to taste a sip.

You can't fight the sands of time, but while the young'uns may still step aside at the door, be wary that with age, your risk profile morphs to Stupid. If you're lucky, you might just lower it to cleverness, but there's no fool like an Old Fool.

Be wily early, be careful later. Big Bucks is the over-40s promise and it can be true. Over-50 seems to be a holding pattern – of doing better but not much new. Over-60 is the slippery zone: the wiliness must be embraced.

If you're pushing towards senior status, be careful how you manage opportunities when they're merely temptations wrapped up in promises. You should know by now that everyone has limited luck and yours might be on the thin side when your head is surrounded by a whitening halo.

Yes, we get smart too late. Stay sharp.

28.

Asking the impossible leaves resentful obligations

Pushing your own limitations implies that you have some skin in the game. Pushing someone else's luck where there is a salaried obligation, is unknown territory. Jumping a stationary rope is a slowly acquired skill for the one being so pushed. Slowly those muscles will grow and get fit. Pushing someone to beyond what is embedded in their self-belief will lead to resentment – with fear of the possible failure and the resulting reputation damage.

Success must weigh heavier than the fall-out of disaster. Why should the CFO risk his future over your hare-brained pre-pay scheme for corporate clients? When in doubt or in push-back mode, it's better to break down the steps to success with evaluation at every benchmark. The best strategy is to couple your own reputation to his if the outcome is uncertain. Together we fly or fail.

The Eternal Fraternal Order of Passive Aggressives is a worldwide phenomenon, and they will actively fight you the moment the seemingly impossible threatens egos, reputations and careers. Taleb's maxim holds for them: Never Risk Big to Win Small. A 20-year career at stake for the dubious glory of a single project? Would you have done it?

29.

SCALING

The most difficult achievement in business is to scale to a magnificent size. It is an art and a skill that is rarer than pink diamonds – it requires a lifelong study to appreciate the intricate dance of hundred perfect steps of the *Ghillie Calum**. It needs an encyclopaedia to explain its intricacies to us mortals.

Forecasting great growth figures is a common expectation and practise. It's as if the doubling of the enterprise is a given every five years, at a realisable growth rate of 14% – or doubling every three-and-a-bit years at a 20% growth rate. Wow. It's possible, and such organic growth is phenomenal, but scaling involves multiples of this.

How do you coherently add scale without significant dilution of ownership or management control and oversight? Scaling isn't a once-off or fortuitous merger or acquisition. It is a strategy with funding, exquisite timing and a coherent execution that implies a jump in size. Scaling requires sacrifice and is beyond mere growth.

Sizing up requires cash, capital, dilution in shares and human capital as well. Adding, multiplying and exponential sizing are freaks of nature – and a few demi-gods dare to jump these crevasses unassisted. Much of scaling involves financial engineering and specialisation beyond just an increase in output. Such *dinosaurisation* has its downsides, as has been widely documented.

The number of JSE-listed corporates in South Africa has dwindled significantly in the last decade, still scaling successes tower over us. Each one has its own impenetrable secrets.

Let's idolise these pinnacles of success and untangle their strategies wherever possible – to learn how they outsmarted and outgrew their fellow piranhas.

Scottish Highland sword dance

30.

CASHING OUT

The Final Irony of Capitalism is the difficulty of cashing in on the potential value of your successful free-market built business. Your expected ten bob may only get offers of around three. That's insulting, and it's a great let-down. Lucky are those souls who timed it right and ejected on a high growth curve. In contrast, the mature, cash-generating cow is somehow less desirable to a potential buyer, especially if the operation is sizeable.

Being asset-rich and cash-poor is the default state of the world that you need to overcome to exit. Lucky you if you can safely pass the enterprise on to your progeny and lay the foundation of a dynasty; but keep in mind the Chinese curse of your heirs not being able to keep up the fortune. They may have inherited your film-star good looks, but not necessarily your business acumen. You will probably find that you need to time your supposed glorious exit as determined by your own age and not that of the enterprise.

The telecoms growth curve peaked in 2014. So too did the pure Information Technology industry. Ditto for businesses in each town and every industry – each has a business cycle that grows to a peak and then withers. Timing your chronological age to coincide with these external lifecycles is an impossibility. Best set up your stall in the market much earlier than you had wanted to.

There is life after super capitalism. It's called benevolence and it is just as satisfying.

31.

SOURCE DISTANCE

Making a decision on the basis of what people tell you instead of from getting to the source is fraught with Pandora's best – letting out all sorts of demons. Everyone between the action and your ear filters according to their own preferences and prejudices. This is a trap of management and it is vital to overcome – a big issue with top management and with you, the CEO.

By the time you hear that shots were fired, this may not have been in the same direction as you are being told. It's often 'Yes, Minister' in its filtered, pampered message that is not the brutal reality that you should face.

Make it your Tom Peters (remember him?) preached mission to devote a day a week to descend into in the trenches, across desks at difficult customers, as close to the frontline as your prickly ego can manage. Be the Napoleon of your industry and let the 'he listens' assurance crescendo as you launch your forays. First-hand listening will build the trust for future bridges.

Listen to the relayed messages, but verify. Yours is not to judge but to understand first. Figure the trends. Find the difficulties. Stay informed. Make decisions on first-hand information. Keep close to the source.

32.

Business staff are socialists, top management is capitalist

Not true you say? Just think about the now-accepted non-free-market systems already operating in your feudal kingdom. Same percentage pay rises. Equal leave days. Give them all the same type of laptops, standardised desks and chairs – a plethora of 'sameness' that shouts 'equality!' on top of Fraternity! and next it may be Liberty! and a roll of drums towards the guillotine?

But what of meritocracy? Equality of access to opportunities *must* override the insidious Equality of Outcomes that underpins dreaded creeping socialism. The minimum requirements now become the maximum advantage, just so that the less useful or less productive units don't feel discriminated against. But they are, and they should be. They get paid less for logical capitalist reasons. Those who over-perform should receive tangible obvious benefits.

Be egalitarian in general, granting equal access at the starting line. Those lounging in the C-Suite shouldn't get automatic benefit just because they are at the top of the pyramid. They should be part of the kudos-for-performance ethos. Reward in public and do that often; chide in private and equally often.

Keep the flag flying of your type of free-market, un-cheating capitalism-for-reward.

33.

Tidy up after meetings

What decisions were made, who will execute them, when will time-lines vest? There are so many decisions, so little time! Meetings mainly end up with almost all possible answers still on the table and generally not enough resources allocated to add what has been decided to the company DNA. Prioritise turning decisions-into-actions.

Hopefully every decision has a stated financial lifetime-profit outcome. This calculation and size will rip apart the important from the merely urgent. Composing decent meeting minutes is a lost art. They *should* be a short reminder of What, Who, When, with a clear, agreed path to the desired Outcome. The benefit of this is that there is, on record, a reminder to all about tasks and obligations.

Do keep in mind that any form of CEO-downwards decision adds to the workload of the victim. Be very clear exactly where in that person's existing task-list you expect that new task to be dropped in, so they can wrestle it to timely completion. Understand why meetings are purgatory for most people – instead of relieving them of the menial or unimportant, as they should do, it is a forum for decisions that add to or up-end their mission to get to your organizational goals. Imagine you asked the right question: "What do you want or need to give up in order to do this new thing?"

That's proper tidying-up and moving ahead.

34.

HOW IMPORTANT IS A GOOD MEMORY?

Sheez. You are generally supposed not only to *know* everything but also to *remember* everything without resorting to any source documents. That may help to explain why you get paid obscenely more than the less gifted and the unlucky. Your memory and insight are expected to operate in four dimensions. Firstly, your knowledge must expand into a wide and ever-growing matrix. You must have a wider grasp of issues than Google – at least for your daily grind.

Secondly, your wisdom must go deep in those areas of anything and everything too. Your memory, in the third part, must recall the past in real time as well as project the future dimension – in width and depth.

The last dimension is virtual: the magic of making sense and simplifying everything so you can lay out understandable actions.

No-one gets this right all the time; Apple's Steve Jobs, billionaire fund manager Ray Dalio and legendary investment guru Warren Buffet stumble – but recover. Your magic dimension must have the practised capacity for analysis, recovery, re-thinking in vibrant alternatives. And then repeat.

You need to remember this always – that's good memory.

35.

DON'T GET DISTRACTED BY THE EXCEPTION

You probably hated Stats in your MBA, like many other sufferers of exponential abstract thinking. The normal distribution, degrees of freedom and fat tailed distribution – and then the Mann-Whitney U-test. Jogged your memory?

Here's how you simplify the abstract for your team: the target is the customers in the fat part of the normal curve, and often you have to start at the thin part and eat your way to the centre. In chess, you need to dominate the middle ground and in squash you need to cover the centre-T on court. Go where the money is – the fat middle.

Still, there is an insidious form of miscommunication trying to persuade you otherwise: shouldn't we also be catering for the minority? The long tail, the lost 5%? This is the sick invention of the new Left that is permeating Common Sense everywhere. They say that 'inclusiveness' is more important than choice; that an insistence that 'no one must be left behind' must supersede merit, and that 'diversity' is more important than free association.

Someone may want to convince you in the C-suite to cater for, or to consider, the 'exception'. Stamp this out Charlie, and quickly. Get those clowns out the door; this type of thinking is fundamentally detrimental. Your Vikings need to charge into the thicket of things, not tiptoe fairy-like to the outliers.

Choose the target. Go berserk with all speed. Succeed. Repeat.

36.

Trajectory is reality

Accountancy is a snapshot science of the past. Real life is a projection into tomorrow. You are the Wizard of the Future, almost everything you do is calculated to have an effect on tomorrow and the years thereafter. The trajectory is the revealed reality. Where you encamp now is less important than your general direction; the trajectory of cash, margin, sales, customer numbers, average usage and the like. Where is this enterprise going? Why? What would change the trajectory? Seek plausible and convincing reasons for choosing how you move ahead.

It is easy to swallow and admire the platitudes of how good the current situation is. The trajectories matter – that's where you'll be going unless something changes the vectors pushing it hence.

There is a margin of error, but you had better make fast and long-lasting adjustments to keep the flight smooth and on course, Captain. What would an acceptable margin be? Your Return on Sales is probably less than 5% – let this be a beacon. Keep on testing each assumption that may change the trajectory else it might become embedded false wisdom.

Often complacency is supported by the notion that it's not too bad at the moment, while dangerously disregarding the trajectory. That could be fatal, and often is.

Trajectory is a chilling prophet and it can summons the grim reaper.

37.

Where does the energy flow to?

Management energy, when properly focused, drives outward expansion, but loses its way if that energy is diverted into administration. Do you detest the 'compliance' disease too?. It is an excuse for employing gatekeepers, vetting agents, naysayers and burden-makers. What percentage of corporate time is allocated to 'house-keeping'? Why? What activities are high-yield and which are low? Growth or maintenance – which is decisive?

It's great to tidy up and dot the i's but this is a secondary priority and not EVER the primary one. Get the ammo correct in terms of, say, the perfect Agreement, Quote, Brochure, and so on – and then go and engage in the fight. Test and measure relentlessly. Where does your hard-fought margin disappear into expenses? The supply lines are crucial, but they are not the objective.

Let's guess more than 80% of time and 50% of emoluments are sacrificed on the altar of Correctness and Order. Think of it as a jealous mother hen who demands rule-following – instead of food-searching. You pay generally by the hour, unfortunately not by output. Is this the right way to operate?

Re-direct the energy into accumulation and progression; you can only wash a car when it's parked and you would rather be eating miles than shine resting stationary.

38.

Few think, the rest want to believe

As an Unconventional CEO, you need to engage memory (see above) and persuasion to get your Best and Brightest to do the same. They might outthink you in their specialities, but generally they would rather believe in your thinking – partly because they're not used to jumping out of the box and partially because it's hard to come up with alternatives. It's both difficult and dangerous.

It's easier and probably a lot safer for them to believe in your ideas. They may want to add accessories to your Hot-rod, but few will propose an electric airplane instead of the existing transport. It is your vehicle; they are coming along for the ride and they want to believe it is the best way forward.

The main source of today's Problems are yesterday's Solutions. Those were the previous ideas of what the fix was going to accomplish. Probably your ideas too? While the thinking B&B's are being encouraged, they need to believe that their ideas will be delivered into a receptive and nourishing medium. Even so, these new-borns may then perhaps be sacrificed on the altar of something better – probably from your musings.

The foot soldiers must constantly be encouraged to keep spawning little devils that will challenge the Good to become much Better. They believe in you and as Caesar said of yon Cassius – he thinks too much, such men are dangerous.

The CEO as an evangelical is alive and well. You need not shout from the pulpit of the boardroom – but yes, do make the daily 'house calls' to keep their faith.

39.

INTEREST VS DIVIDEND YIELD

Do the divvies exceed the interest rate on risk-free savings?

Does the return on capital/NAV exceed the interest rate on risk-free savings?

How else do you test your own performance from the viewpoint of your risk-taking shareholders?

These may appear quaint questions in a world doused in trivia and kept on the boil with fancy terminology. The long and short of it is whether the risk taken with, say, $100,000 of net assets is worth it. Assume they can get a 9% risk -free yield on a Money Market fund, so how does this stack up against the dividend yield on your company's net assets?

Not all companies return a competitive rate – and that's without taking all the risks of the business into account. I'd say the risk should at least add 50% to the Money Market return to lure-in, and then hold on to, an investor.

Does your entity return 15% dividend yield? Thought not.

Does your entity at least have a return on capital of 15% – when you don't pay dividends? Perhaps not either.

Then how do you convince your risk-taking shareholders to applaud your magnificent salary in the light of their oh-so-easy alternative?

Hmm..

40.

TERMS OF REFERENCE INSTEAD OF POSITION DESCRIPTION

Is there a difference? Let me make a case. Consider the cart and the horse. The Terms of Reference detail the outcomes that need to be achieved and the resources that need to be allocated to get there. As an example, how do you ensure a positive cash-flow structure? It needs a mechanism. It needs an overseer/implementer. How do you budget for less than 0.5% of debtors outstanding per month? Start by laying out the outcomes that are required. What actions are needed to achieve this?

Can a single person fulfil all this? As the company grows, is one person still sufficient to produce the required outcomes? The cart needs to be pulled at a certain rate, over a required distance and at a set frequency. What you need may be two mules to cope at month's end, but just one pony after that. Be specific with the goals and how to reach them, think it through, and keep on refining how you are progressing, and whether you have the right people in the right places. These are the terms of reference.

Finding things for the horse to do is Peter Principle stuff where work expands into time available; the desired outcomes must be lined-up, and then the process of getting there must be described in measurable terms.

What's an acceptable deviation?

What is 'lights shot out' performance?

How the shooting should be done is an ongoing debate, not a position description.

Defining the tasks around available people is how the small enterprise starts out. At size and at speed it requires sophistication of the requirements that will lead to efficiency, not the adding of people while dividing the workload into position descriptions.

41.

KEEP YOUR FORM, LIKE IN SWIMMING

Swimming the crawl stroke, needs 80% of your effort to overcome inertia and water resistance and is a useful metaphor for leadership. For better performance, you require more efficiency and less power, more endurance and less splash, calmness and a deep knowledge of what's required to perform well.

Your style may be the butterfly or you may team up for a medley, but the same approach applies. Business, as in life, is for the slow-twitch muscles, not a quest for the burst of blood to the head. Most importantly, you need to keep your form even if – and especially when – you tire. Extra twitches, losing the rhythm and unnecessary body movements are detrimental; that's not what you trained for.

Similarly, all sorts of burdens may grind you down and wobble your execution. It's then time to concentrate all the more, to keep your form, to hold your pace and tempo. Keep your style. Keep the end in mind. Your consistency and confidence keep your troops in awe and psyched up.

Good form is less tiring physically and takes less mental effort, too. You're used to it, unconsciously competent and comfortably confident. Do not get disrupted; take the waves and eddies in your stride and put on a display of calm and confident unruffledness.

42.

PROFESSIONAL OR PERSONAL?

When a situation initiates a cross from professional to personal, it becomes time to fight or to go. Keep this rule: never confuse your professional relationship with fellow professionals with your personal like or dislike of them. They don't have to like you to work there and you do not want to give them any personal reason excuse to bring out the pitchforks.

Your talented help is each hired for their professional skills. They may want to drag you to court for perceived wrongs – that's their right and you must never begrudge them that. Let the impartial law find what's right or wrong; your calm and inspiring demeanour must never slip.

Do not allow any personal pettiness among your troops. It is, at all times, the greatest priority to professionally apply skills to the common outcome. We party at home; we professionalise at the office. Personally, I never entertain any co-workers or even directors after-hours, and certainly not at home.

However much they are liked or not is always irrelevant. It's how much I respect their abilities in their chosen, or appointed, position. Never show your personal like or dislikes for people except, perhaps, when it comes to their professional behaviour. Even then make it extremely clear: this is not personal; it is only professional.

43.

The knowledge gap between manager and subordinates

Knowledge … or skills? Frequently the subordinate has more skill at tasks than his or her manager – who may have done those tasks well enough to advancing upwards. What should the approach be to harbouring and sharing knowledge. Does it go upstream as well as flowing down from on-high? What often separates the manager from the worker – speaking in the broadest terms – is the definition, the concept, of the outcome.

The accountant may have a balancing set of accounts as an outcome, while the financial director may measure the number of journal entries that fixed misallocations, or aim to get the cashflow done as soon as possible. Both have the skills to do entries and to balance the books; but the intention of the FD is not aligned with that of the accountant. The accountant is 'doing the job'. In the bigger scheme, is the 'job and the skill of doing it' the best tool for accomplishing the FD's desired outcome?

Thus the knowledge gap is the incomplete knowledge of the accountant of what exactly his boss sees as his own outcome. Both types of knowledge gaps must be overcome. Today's accountant is tomorrow's potential FD. Train and equip the grafters with more insights and deeper understanding of what pushes the upstream's buttons.

44.

Too much aiming

You need to pull the trigger often, not just aim, aim, aim. Making plans or thinking through strategy is good and necessary, but only action can bring the desired changes. Lead from the front in good and bad times, but do lead.

Procrastination, waiting for the perfect timing and the correct strategy, is no good. How did you ever learn to ride a bike other than by getting on, falling off, and getting on again? Eventually you can pedal along more times than you crash. Make the decisions, implement, revisit, refine, redirect. Too much aiming and too little firing is not going to help you to hang the carcasses around the camp in the hunting season.

With practice, you will get better at firing, but you won't improve by just thinking about practise. Being good enough is a good beginning. Almost no-one ends up marrying their first crush, so heed the lesson of practicing to get better by action. Mistakes? Of course. Fixing them? Naturally. Learning from the fallout? Absolutely. Do not miss the opportunities. Fire!

45.

TAKE THE FIRST PAY CUT

Symbolism can have a massive psychological impact, and it is sadly in decline as a science and an art. Wear a tie, or no tie? Don the light blue shirt or the black tee? Park your Porsche at the entrance, or somewhere less prominent?

You should be the one to publicly take the first pay cut when austerity hits. Order first but order modestly at lunch – thus the symbolism continues, time after time. Armies wear their step-outs, give medals, raise flags, stand to attention and soldiers sport army haircuts. Define your brigade, give them a sense of entitlement and symbols to match.

Cohesion breeds co-operation and reciprocity, conformity makes interaction smoother. Think about the negative symbols and structures which abound. Who's filtering your reality? Who may step in unannounced? Who is sucking up and who is being difficult?

You need to harness the energy that now goes into playing up; channel it into improved professional behaviour. In dealing with people, send signs, make symbols, and even give martyr signals – firing for untoward behaviour and unacceptable results. Be aware that respect and awe for you will serve the company better than if you are merely liked or admired.

46.

THE DIFFICULT ONES

Yes, they are there, and for good but sometimes unfathomable reason. Autopilot flying is easy, but you may want a less compliant personality in charge when the going gets tough. Why is this? If there is creative discontent, frustration over imposed limits – you may have a hot potato hiding a valuable diamond in his hand.

The required art is to channel and use that vigour, obstinacy and frustration. OK, maybe give them at least one chance to put that energy into look-at-me-now winning behaviour; or else you may just have a sizzling dud instead of a live firecracker. Corralling cats is a good metaphor for this, but your managerial fun is compounded by an array of difficult and clashing personalities, and more than one may be evident in the same person.

If you have kids you know the drill; fairness to everything but some individual idiosyncrasies warrant jealous attention. That borderline fit-in vs absolute cowboy isn't cast in stone; it's a line drawn in the sand that you are being dared to cross, and vice versa. The wind blows and the mark changes; it's time to go toe to toe and redraw it.

Yes, you as the Boss will win the contest, however exhausting it is, but you'll appreciate being able to call upon that unbottleable vigour once a live target for destruction appears. Ever hunted with a proper greyhound? Go find and watch a video of this and be assured that your patience with the Difficult Ones may pay off, even if you currently feel they're more shoe-chewing mastiff at present.

47.

REDUCTION FOR CONTROL

Is change required for improvements? Often progress is accomplished through reduction and not by addition. Less can mean more. Take fewer steps and you will see more coherent processes. It is change – by doing less.

What in your magnificent capitalist behemoth can be eliminated to accomplish progress? What would function better if there is less of it, fewer handovers in a process or at least coherently simplified?

Let the reduction process begin! Let the experimentation start. In reduction, the failure can easily be rolled-back after lessons are learned. Think of poetry: the haiku and sonnet are both fixed in shape. The haiku has a set form and standard. It is 5, 7 and then again 5 syllables over three lines. It is measurable, it is standardized, the outcome is controlled:

> King on golden throne.
> Deep bowing peasants marvel -
> powerful alone.

This haiku is 'correct' but not necessarily good or soothing on the ear. It is a good start and now the improvement can commence, let the experimentation proceed.

Reducing corporate actions and processes like the words and syllables to get a memorable poem is easier in form than in beauty. In order to qualify as and to compare to others, the poem form is standardised and controlled. Once so modelled, it can be measured and compared.

So too your reporting: from setting standards to achieving beautiful results. Your control is built on the measurements done on these standards agreed and set. If is measurable, it can be managed. If it can be managed, it can be controlled.

If done right, it sounds like this – even translated from Japanese it is a joy.

> These useless dreams, alas!
> Over fields of wilted grass
> Winds whisper as they pass
> -*Onitsure (1661)*

48.

KNOWING WHAT TO DO
AND NOT DOING IT

This is a cardinal sin. Worth firing someone for. Inexcusable. A let-down of a whole career built on doing things well. Your conviction must carry you, and when it fails, share the question but remain solely accountable for the answer. Of course, if you don't know what to do, you had better ask for advice – instead of guessing what your next job will be if you get it wrong.

Practise 'knowing' in your mind, or better still with a mentor over some good coffee. Practise the doing daily and in view of the staff.

Teenagers have such 'phases' of knowing and not doing; and that's the timeframe of life where it belongs and should remain. You must face the music, heed the call, do what's necessary as you realise that the alternative would be knowing without doing.

Ditto for your people when you realise the same. Passive aggres-sive behaviour is common and can be rationalised away as being too busy, or the like. In reality it is an active choice to disrespect and subvert the command structure. Passive hostility and resistance to commands will exasperate the person who is expecting action.

Such not-doing can lead to undoing; it must be diagnosed early and mercilessly stamped out, or the un-doer should be released to go and wreck your opposition, pronto.

49.

WHEN SPECIALISATION BECOMES COUNTERPRODUCTIVE

Seeing a task through to fulfilment begets good emotional feedback. Specialisation means chunking the problem into various skill areas and often this improves the speed of execution as well as the efficiency from the higher skills applied to the solution. Yet interrupting the flow of accolades depersonalizes the cogs in your well-oiled profit machine. It's your particular skill to find out who hogs the glory and who does the heavy-lifting without the rewarding back-pats.

Since Adam Smith kicked off the industrial revolution by punting labour specialisation, it has been the progress mantra for almost 250 years. Allow your keen teams some ability to grow sideways as a better base to enable you all to grow upwards. What extra skills, what new experiences and what new perspectives can they add to their CVs while you harvest the benefits? Who might blossom in a changed role? Who will be shown up for being a hoarder of some unshared and delinquent responsibilities? Should your champs become more generalists?

Yes. Generalist insects are more intelligent than specialized ones – think ants vs ticks. The smartest insects are the generalists who do not repeat tasks in a set order and ants rank pretty high-up in the critter IQ shoot-out. Workers ants understand their tasks and are innovative in finding solutions for the colony. Bees, too – and they are beset with life-threatening situations in finding elusive food sources. Ticks? They suck blood.

Humans have an important commonality, described as the 'social brain hypothesis'. Its proponents believe that living in a group pressures individuals to become smarter to ensure their survival, rather than those smart individuals choosing to live in groups for survival.

The corporate colony demands effort translated into results. The business hive sends its workers to gather nectar. There is something to be learned from generalist group behaviour. It swarms around you during office hours.

You would hope that by developing a greater percentage of the 100 billion neurons each person brings to work in a caffeine-soaked readiness, you could have them accomplish more and see wider smiles at the go-home rush.

Tough calls on what to spur to greatness in whom, but you earn big bucks for being so wise and wonderful, so narrow the eyes and find who's being screwed over in the trophy stakes.

Rethink the compartmentalizing for efficiency. Some positions have all the luck. By adding responsibilities to foster more generalization you can help blow the fairy dust a bit wider.

50.

THINKING VS JUDGING

Easy? Judging gets you to a conclusion on which you must act. That's the easy part. Thinking – and thinking things through – is an alien concept in a world of *ersatz** conclusions on a trot. Henry Fonda's *12 Angry Men* is a film about jury duty and it is of enormous importance to watch. It should lay an extra lane on your road and boost your navigation to more equitable conclusions when you make decisions.

Watching it imparts the folly of a single perspective – which is probably your weakness most of the time. It breaks down the gangster attitude that being a CEO makes one pretty infallible and if you ever made a mistake – well they were wrong about that too. Whom do you trust to bounce the facts off? How soon do you reach a conclusion, relying on the meagre facts presented?

Be gracious when you're correct; be humble when you're wrong and quick to set things right. Some decisions are easy to fix and you need to overthink those that will not be so easy; remember that you're judge, jury and executioner in your office. Think and act in a way that is impartial, professional, unemotional, rational – the list can go on but the message is that you must engage the frontal cortex before, and hopefully instead of the reptilian judging brain stem.

Flying off the handle and jumping to conclusions are exercises that can be regretted later, at leisure, and you don't have the time to repair or retract. Being snappy may be a great compliment to your actionable self, hard to undo and sorting out any mess should be shared among other jurors, conspirators or management and board members.

Judging is final. Think first.

---

* Ersatz is the German term for 'instant' and denotes something inferior'

51.

Don't use conventional words to push unconventional ideas

In your war of persuasion to get your *kamikazes* to do your bidding, many factors must be compiled to compete for the honour or you will risk the dishonour of failing to move the troops. Your messianic presence in appearing before the jaded lifers is your best shot. You have honed the message. The advantages of following this new path are clear.

The approaching toil and suffering will be rewarded. There's treasure waiting at the rainbow's end. Your knights need to remember your message on their journey. Few will write it down or record it; all will interpret it through their own language filters.

Your words may not have the same meaning to each of them, even though they were delivered in your known corporate language. (Throughout these pages you'll find invented words. No apology for that.)

It is time to earn your legacy and boil up their adrenaline. You must devise and use some images and words that are new, memorable and that can anchor the rallying cry. Give your project a great name. Define its personal outcomes in detail. Describe the horrific sacrifices ahead. Detail the logistics, and promise support that will endure until victory, and beyond.

You had better be creative, and perhaps seek good help for the unconventional language, words and images to use as, from the outset, they will stand apart from how you normally communicate. In time, the entire business must migrate to these images as the re-invention of the tasks ahead.

Leif Eriksson did that with 'Greenland' – that forsaken snow and glacier-covered almost-continent and Vikings still live there 1200 years later. Floki Vilgerdarson chose 'Iceland' to keep other settlers away; and if Leif called his fief 'Iceland North' he would NOT have moved those 200 families from the Scandinavian coast.

Stir up the hormones, spike the wanderlust, whet the appetite for booty in glowing and memorable terms. Calling it "Project Daedalus – to fly to where None have Gone" is so much better than "New Product Launch, 16th of September". Lubricate the salivaries of your tigers, give them reasons to proudly smash into the future.

52.

BEWARE OF PRECONCEIVED NOTIONS ABOUT YOUR COMPETITORS

Do you know your customers better than you know your competitors? Probably, as your spies will lament, it's hard to know what they're up to. Really? In an age of websites, tweets, LinkedIn, corporate PR and the ability to interview their hotshot for possible employment?

Do you keep up to date with their progress – what works and what doesn't – or do you remain oblivious, just focused on plugging your own version of what customers should buy? Worse – do you have an armoury of one-liner disparaging descriptions of all the other vendors? Gathering market intelligence is unfortunately often seen as an tedious process. It is not. It is an integral part of what determines your rise and fall.

Acting as a forceful competitor means vying against the pack for the one set of eyes and cheque-writing hands out there. This is hard work and the results will often be demotivating, especially if you find that others may be beating your best effort with their insolence at your expense. Knowing what the customer wants will ensure that you focus on the money flow, and if the flow is not your way, you had better figure out why.

Keep up to date with the dynamics that threaten you.

53.

OBSTACLES VS CHALLENGES

It's pretty decisive to know the difference here, as your people will need to know these words – unlike in Orwell's *1984*, where a lack of descriptors prevents anyone from thinking properly about the real meanings. An Obstacle is something that needs to be removed, hopefully once and for all, in order to advance. Farmers need to get crop financing in place. A majority is needed for a Law to be passed, A fallen tree blocks the road.

Tackling an obstacle means dedicating sufficient resources just to get action, else it will be White Flag time. Define your Obstacles to improvement, to success; work out what you will need in order to break through – and then calculate the time, cost and resources needed to overcome; else let it go.

Some fights you can win on your own. Others either need different and more troops or are best left for other suckers – or until you have come up with a better plan. Remember that you're being paid to *be* that plan, comrade-in-arms. No pressure! Unlike Obstacles, Challenges are the other stuff, the niggles that continuously get in the way of a fast-moving team. These challenges are never-ending and hopefully, if you are deserving of your weighty salary – also never repeat themselves. Classify the difficulties: are they once-off eyebrow-raising impediments, or brow-furrowing whack-a-moles that keep cropping up to be dealt with?

54.

DIFFICULT VS COMPLICATED VS COMPLEX

When asked about the most complex or complicated issues in their jobs, most staff will define the merely difficult. Let's cut this concept of "difficult" into its parts.

It is merely difficult when it can be resolved by Management. Why would a task be 'difficult' to accomplish?

It might be any: "I don't have the skills, either professional or technical."

Or: "I don't have the authority to do what needs to be done."

Or: "I don't have the resources, budget, staff, process or clarity."

These are known issues and answers exist and are routine.

Solving the Complicated is beyond mere daily management. It involves known elements but the outcomes are tricky and not guaranteed correct or desired. The complicated needs more than the usual Management resources, it dives into Nerd territory because of the uncertainty of outcomes,

It also requires specialists and ever-advancing procedures to keep getting things right and correct. Selling is complicated, fixing software is complicated, modelling new product outcomes is complicated. Strategies and tactics can be honed to overcome the complicated.

The Complex involves unknowns and is difficult to reduce to a recipe, rule or process. Elements change, unforeseen consequences reign, the real word intrudes mercilessly to stir up the results. The Complex needs wide understanding versus the Complicated's need for deep understanding. Complex is the New Territory, the start of the process of fixing these problems are unclear and so is the correct path. Finding a hacker-proof communication system is complex. Political solutions are complex.

Difficult: *Well-known issues. You know what to do and the outcome of each action is known and certain. Kick ass inside the box.*

Complicated: *Known issues. You are certain what to do, but the outcome is uncertain. Shuffle the tools in the box with systems, processes and 'recipes'.*

Complex: *Unknown issues. You are uncertain what to do to and the outcome of each effort is uncertain. Think outside the box.*

Difficulties are daily drudges. Complex is what will keep you on sleeping tabs, Complication keeps the minions on ulcer meds.

After all you don't get those gastric excitations – you give them.

55.

Illegal vs unlawful vs immoral vs inappropriate

It may sound like semantics, but it is valuable to know the differences between these terms. Here's a short primer to help.

Illegal is when actions violate a law – statutory, regulation ordinance or rule. A breach is punishable by a set of actions (defined penalties) after one is found guilty. This is straightforward – illegal action means breaking the law, and it has its consequences.

When it is **unlawful** – although this is confusingly used as a synonym for Illegal – it denotes things that are not correct in law i.e. contracts or actions that are contrary to policy – human or divine – which are not authorised in law, or are prohibited. "It's Unlawful" is often the cry when things should be illegal but aren't, when there's behaviour that shouldn't happen and may lead to an illegal action.

The **immoral** is subjective – defined as contrary to accepted practises in terms of interpersonal behaviour. Some mainstream religions exempt their adherents from cheating the non-believers. The victims will cry "immoral", but the slope is slippery. Good behaviour and expectations are best agreed on in a multi-cultural, generally unprincipled, world of business. In general, your Talent must know that you err on the side of conservatism and better that there be a wide margin around it too.

Flirting round the coffee machine? Needlessly making a creditor wait? Reneging on a delivering a freebee to a customer? These can be made into moral or immoral issues but you had better call them minimum standards of behaviour. Puritan, above-board, inoffensive: set your business principles in unforgiving stone to honour your customers, suppliers and staff with the best of moral, lawful and legal business.

Finally, what is **inappropriate**? This is situation-dependent, and much more civilised. Can your techs bring zero-alcohol beer to work? It's not Illegal, Unlawful or Immoral. But it's Inappropriate, like low-cut dresses, smelly shirts and the like. It's your call.

56.

WILD IDEAS AND CONSERVATIVE EXECUTION

This most interesting observation thrown my way and taken as a compliment – is to have wild ideas with conservative implementations. There may be some wisdom in restraining the impulses and tame them for productive use.

In one my several perceptions of the circle of Life there is an interplay:

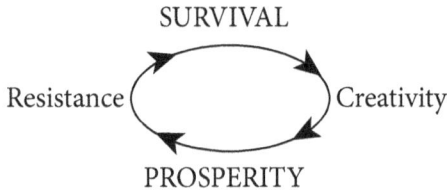

SURVIVAL

Resistance $\bigcirc$ Creativity

PROSPERITY

Graduating from Survival to Prosperity is a lifetime's work. Creativity underlies the process of striving, working, risking and succeeding. Those with limited developed creativity may miss the main route to reward.

Crazy ideas become mainstream after success. Crazy ideas need careful implementation due to the many new and risky factors and uncertain outcomes they bring. Drug lords can have an enforced execution policy (I think) but yours will be more tippy-toe; learn as you go. Your 'conservative' will probably draw deeper breaths from other lesser mortals.

Tie down every phase of execution so that you can reverse an unsuccessful action. Generate options but stick to the recipe: newness is its own seduction but it can unseat you. Be careful but decisive, creative but resist threats – or else it is back to survival mode.

Think comic book; write textbook. That is the interplay.

57.

MESSY STARTS AND MESSY ENDINGS

The Perfect Plan is just that until the start button is pushed. As Prussian military strategist Helmuth von Moltke said, even the best strategy doesn't survive the first contact. The plan disappears when the first shot is fired. Business is messy and your job is to keep it clean – but new starts require cat-herding skills.

New ventures, even in the established organization have messy starts, often turn nasty and are inevitably disappointing as it takes longer, costs more and falls short of expectations. It's nature at its best – birth and death are dangerous and brutal. Even moving office is a untidy process of surprises and disappointments. Winding up, undoing, re-doing, rethinking and realigning are normal and noisily messy.

Once the rhythm of the business is disturbed, either by change to the new or an ending of the old, the recipe goes missing. Expect this, and welcome it – as your boundaries may have become soft and flabby, your emergency thinkability a tad rusty, and your reactions treacly slow. The messy brings out the unvarnished person like all stress situations do.

There is a brief moment in time for you to scrutinise your soon-to-change world while the pawpaw is arcing towards the fan – who will catch and who will duck the mess? Messy situations ought to be pre-empted by Plans B, C and more; nothing is more worthless than redoubling your same effort on something which refuses to bring success. Winching-out is needed when pushing forward has failed in the mud puddle. Messy endings are not where you want to end up but they occur too often to ignore. Try to clean up as you go along.

58.

Relief vs ecstasy

Here's a little personal test of stress levels: how do you and your people react to success – with relief or with a burst of ecstasy? This is simple, but telling. The confidence level is reflected in the stress level; these are joined at the hip.

The higher the confidence, the more the exultation to feed that confidence – and that is what you should promote, encourage and cheerlead. Those deep sighs of relief are not what you want to hear after the Gold Medal ceremony. That would be indicative of a deep and disturbing tendency towards hope, instead of the deep-rooted 'I-Can'.

This outcome either shows fear or unpreparedness. Fear must be conquered – by proper preparation and not by oodles of hope. You welcome courage by the spadesful – true, but sweat by the bucket-load is more important.

59.

ITERANT DESIGN

In the aircraft industry, iterant design is the nightmare. The landing-gear designers build the lightest undercarriage. The wing designers make wings a little larger for a bigger payload. The undercarriage is not strong enough, so it's upgraded. Now the plane is too heavy, and the wings get lengthened. The plane is now too heavy for the landing-gear … And so, the game of iterant design runs on and on.

Sounds familiar? This is the name of the my-department-first fun that the whole company can play. Who's On First – like Abbott & Costello (please find and watch that!). Who's more important, who gets the blame, and who gets the funds?

Iterant design is often the Gordian knot that need to be cut, not untangled. Stride in like Alexander and subdue the egos in motion. It's your insight – and it better be correct – as you are in the role of Solomon, and your wisdom must rise above the collective opinions and facts.

How? King Arthur them at a roundtable, and ask the questions and prods until there is consensus on what is absolute mostest important, what is less most important and so on.

You'll also spot the constraints in the process; who is *ottering* the flow of the stream by building a dam empire? You are challenged to undo the egos in the room. YOU are King Ego and there must be a respectful murmur from everyone giving up a little bit of their own for the Greater Good.

60.

THE MAGIC PHRASE

Beyond the great lubricator of the heart-felt 'Please' and the sincere 'Thank You' while looking into the eyes, lies the real Magic Phrase in your management emergency kit: "How can I help?' It can send chills of horror or spasms of delight down the spinal cord, depending on the circumstances and the tone of delivery.

It's probably the best doorbuster around. These are also the most reassuring words with which Competent can reassure your troubled psyche. I recollect Herr Götschke's story when he met the *Führer* as a Chancellery Guard in 1945: "How can I help you, soldier?" asked the Nazi leader. Better food resulted, but one look in the blue eyes as he was being asked invigorated him for life.

Perhaps it may not be your idea of how to conquer the world, but these words, asked with open ears could not only endear you as the wonderful and caring uber-capitalist you've become, but may also uncover the details that look like insurmountable Andes from the toiler's perspective.

My bet is that the answers will mostly be mundane and fixable with a snap of the fingers, thus burnishing your reputation with very little effort. The catch? When should you ask this? My take is it should be in that moment of personal connection, when trust is glowing like the voltage from a Van de Graaf generator*, or something close to it. This is a personal question, eye to eye, mano a mano, and getting this right may solidify the water under your walking feet for those feeling the love.

---

* *Van der Graaf generator produces spectacular electrostatic discharges through its metal globe*

61.

LIKE A TOP CHESS PLAYER, KNOW MANY POSITIONS

What are your standard moves? How do your people rate and respond to them? You don't know your stock reactions? Submit yourself to be roasted* by your staff and learn about Robert Burns' lines:

> O wad some Pow'r the giftie gie us, to see oursels as
> ithers see us!

Roasting is a tongue-in-cheek commentary on your way of doing the management thing. How do you react to bad news? To disappointment? How do you show elation, if at all? Anger? Do you use stock words to praise or convey bad news? Are you a cardboard caricature when motivating others or are you a Top Gun Maverick? It's important to know yourself if the real you is the one known to all. The Scottish bard concludes that poem to a louse:

> It wad frae mony a blunder free us, An' foolish notion.

You would need a little deviation from your accustomed style if you want to emphasise newness or to introduce a new incentive; a little less predictability when the exceptional ones need your emotional confirmation of their greatness.

Ask your Better or Other Half – and do more than listen; take out your notebook, make notes and use them for future reference. You must be a stoic leader who is pretty dependable and predictable – but only up to a point. Know your positions, know when to innovate them, and know when to insert your ideas into previously perfectly-working models.

" *A roast is a form of humour where the guest of honour is subjected to jokes made at his expense, intended to amuse the audience.*

Watch and learn from the great orators and the comics for more moves. You need to be memorable from time to time. Less is better and a silent smile often conveys different interpretations to your audience, as opposed to opening your mouth and dispelling all uncertainty. A little unpredictability can keep them on their toes.

Be aware, know your moves and their impact on the suspecting and unsuspecting. Chameleon, you aren't expected to walk the Smarties box by the hour while changing spots; it's your ability to know and know what and when a change is required to un-jade the lidded eyes following your hovering cloud around.

62.

The multipreneur

Do you dare to step up to the challenge?

This is your ongoing quest – new voices of the Sirens* calling you towards the rocks – or towards greater victories. You're a potential multipreneur – else you would not be steering the ship. Multipreneurship is not in your Job Description, it is the unspoken expectation to carefully do what is required but unknown in your journey towards the riches that owners expect. That will require being an entrepreneur – several times over. If it's your own business you're running, you will recognize yourself here.

At worst, becoming entrereneurial is starting something brand new and uncomfortable to your set of skills. At best it is extending an existing line of products. Every story is the same: problem, options and solution. Sometimes it looks like opportunity, choices and completion. Beware the temptation, commitments and consequences. Your ability to see the risk and reward relationship, the smooth shift of staff into new modes of business and the acceptance of the new stepchild into the family will be tested, however small your new baby that gets delivered. It comes with the proverbial nappies, howling for attention and the jealousies and sleep deprivation for the family.

You cannot sit on your hands too long while opportunities drift by. Sometimes you should just do that until numbness sets in. It is the multi-disciplinarian in you that will help with the choices. Buying a new data center? The builder in you should be costing the new ducting and fiber trenching needed long before price negotiations commence. Adding acreage to your existing soya farming? The

---

* The Sirens called to Odysseus to change his course in irresistibly song. He escaped the deadly temptation by having himself tied to the mast as they sailed past..

engineer in you should be calculating available grid electricity for the additional pivots. What skills are in your team to filter the risks? What experience of similar enterprises sit around your managers' tables?

Here's where the 'dare' part becomes relevant. All civilizations rise then fall, either to Assyrian oblivion (often) or to Greek adaptation in ensuing centuries (rare). Multipreneurship is a choice, a personal philosophy and a ratchetable adroitness. Use it or lose it.

> **Brutus:**
> *There is a tide in the affairs of men.*
> *Which, taken at the flood, leads on to fortune;*
> *Omitted, all the voyage of their life*
> *Is bound in shallows and in miseries.*
> *On such a full sea are we now afloat,*
> *And we must take the current when it serves,*
> *Or lose our ventures.*

Brutus and Julius didn't part on good terms, but there's much wisdom in this section from J. Caesar. Misery is not in your plan, greatness is.

Dare to be great. One step at a time, but a proper one. Multipreneur your way to the stars.

63.

Pushiness

It's said about Elon that he is extremely pushy. Ditto the incomparable Jobs. Also Edison, and possibly most of the business greats who wouldn't wait for things to run their 'natural' course. There is a hostile world out there encroaching on all that you have lined up. Time's a wasting and tomorrow never comes. Carpe diem – whatever excuse you deem necessary for motivation to exalted levels of performance and excellence. The impossible is only a historic concept for the successful.

In short, pushiness is a requirement for great success. You require the extraordinary, the unthinkable and the astonishing. Your front-liners can deliver and you need to remind them that they can, and then do so by the hour. Unreasonableness is in the eye of the beholder. Henry Ford had three non-experts develop the continuous glass manufacturing process. 'I took a great personal interest in its success' he wrote. Read that to mean 'I personally pushed them to and beyond the limits continuously'. Give resources, give praise, recognition, advancement, more resources but do not compromise your expectations. Be clear, be unreasonable but be consistent.

Pushiness can be exasperating, irritating and demotivating to those pushed. Like the great forces of nature, it culls the unworthy and rewards the best. Make it an art form.

64.

Planners vs. Problem solvers

This may be contrary to your intuition: find those who keep solving problems day by day and get rid of them.

Problem solvers are bad planners, hence their need to become 'indispensable' to the issues at hand. Find the department, the section, the people who are renowned for their thinking-on-their-feet abilities. Evaluate the forward planning done. Evaluate the ability to follow procedures. Find the cause of the multiple problems. It will be mostly the lack of foresight and planning. Eliminate the stress it causes to those around them.

Expedient problem solving is a deep skill that must be used to overcome the surprises, not the disasters. The latter are known risks, badly circumvented and new blood with wide vision will be needed. Test your people thus. You want less squeaky wheel problem solving, more smooth ride accomplishment.

Do not overlook the real champions, those that make things look easy. They will have time to wrestle new and impossible tasks to ground. Good planning is in their genes and makes for predictable execution. They should be itemized on your Balance Sheet.

65.

FOCUS

There is too much time in your day, too many hours of not doing the correct things.

If you disagree you may have a problem with focus. Of course you can do almost everything and do it well. You shouldn't. You should watch it being done better than you can do it. You need to constantly re-think and re-plan your day, your position, your actions, your outcomes and your success by the hour. You need to understand what you must focus on above all else, notwithstanding the interruptions of daily business.

What should your primary focus be? What is the only thing important enough that you should spend your entire day on, which you shouldn't delegate and which will determine the ongoing superlative success of what you are doing? That is what you must focus on.

What should that focus be for every single position in your organization? How will that focus be defined in every person's position description? Is this even possible?

Extraordinary, intense and unwavering focus is the foundation of the quest for the superlative business. It is the extreme focus on what is most important business ground rule to succeed. For example:

For the data center business: <u>uninterruptible service</u>. The focus on uninterruptible determines the power sourcing, the multiplicity of connectivity, the unbreachable security, the choice of equipment, the operations and then the choice of quality client selection as the first principle.

For the farming finance business: <u>finding leasable land for successful farmers</u>. This drives the risk down, eases supplier credit extension, increases the potential for higher yields and grows long-term relationship. This is not the focus one would expect from a financier.

For the marine diamond dredging business: <u>continuous operation in proven high yield pockets of diamonds</u>. The vessels, methodologies, crew and operations are designed around 'continuous'. The choice of location, the geophysical information, the tools in use are chosen around 'continuous'. When weather, access, visibility, breakages, rotation, sampling and onboard processing limitations are overcome, the process becomes 'continuous' and can be applied in high yield pockets. The focus is how to improve and sustain 'continuous' into 'high yield' with the resulting payback on the enormous cost of equipment.

For the property development business: <u>acquiring inexpensive land that meets the required potential</u>. The profit is made in the land acquisition, all else is at market related prices including the eventual sale. What is 'inexpensive'? The intended purpose of the land determines that. Shopping center zoning yields more than housing, multiple story dwellings yield more than zoning for schools. Understanding the potential makes the focus easy.

What is your constant unconventional CEO business focus? Are all other positions aligned to your focus and are they all eyes and ears to help you see?

66.

Have the courage to resist the Laughter

Really? It's the snickering when you're out of sight that you should overcome. Why would your own seemingly-loyal adjutants make mirth of your actions? Only when they are not convinced of your leadership. You're being belittled for your ideas, actions or for just being you.

Being exceptional gets you to the top, being a thick-skinned exceptional keeps you there. Your ideas are not created to be pleasing for the masses, but to be caviar to the General. Not all your musings will see the light of day or the podium, but it takes courage to keep them coming and to develop, refine, sell, confirm, defend, change and timeously implement those that fit the job.

Without the exercise of thinking, the achievement of implementing will not happen. That most dangerous word, ego, needs to be set aside when inventing the future. If your efforts go unappreciated but your conviction remains, find better soil to plant and prosper.

Companies die much faster than people, and in your time as the Top Dog you will see many shuffling off that mortal coil for the great What-Could-Have-Been in the sky. Your feet are on the ground and moving forward. If the laughter persists or grows too loud, reconsider those historical Italian pantomime characters – the Pierrots, Columbines and Harlequins – as they manifest in the corporate world.

If you cannot laugh with them, it may be time to laugh at them, to love them but leave them as you prepare the afterburners to zoom into the higher stratosphere.

That's you, the Unconventional CEO.

Afterword

Something enjoyable is never a drudge. Sometimes the joy has to be found to convince oneself. I hope that you have read this far and think yourself part of that small and gnarly band of Unconventional brothers.

Welcome!

*9 7 8 1 7 7 6 0 5 6 6 5 1 *